Wild Britain

Bromley

THE LONDON BOROUGH
www.bromley.gov.uk

e and Richard Spilsbury

Please return this item by the last date stamped below, to the library from which it was borrowed.

Renewals
Any item may be renewed twice by telephone or post, provided it is not required by another customer. Please quote the barcode number.

Overdue Charges
Please see library notices for the current rate of charges levied on overdue items. Please note that the overdue charges are made on junior books borrowed on adult tickets.

Postage
Postage on overdue notices is payable

Southborough Library
Southborough Lane
Bromley BR2 8HP
020 8467 0355

2 4 NOV 2014		
15 Dec lun		
3 1 MAR 2018		

Renewals
0333 370 4700
arena.yourlondonlibrary.
net/web/bromley

THE LONDON BOROUGH

21 JUL 12 PO

- 7 OCT 2013

www.heinemann.co.uk
Visit our website to find out more information about Heinemann Library books.

To order:
☎ Phone 44 (0) 1865 888066
📄 Send a fax to 44 (0) 1865 314091
💻 Visit the Heinemann Bookshop at www.heinemann.co.uk to browse our catalogue and order online.

First published in Great Britain by Heinemann Library, Halley Court, Jordan Hill, Oxford OX2 8EJ, part of Harcourt Education Ltd. Heinemann is a registered trademark of Harcourt Education Ltd.

Editorial: Lucy Thunder and Helen Cox
Design: David Poole and Celia Floyd
Illustrations: Alan Fraser and Geoff Ward
Picture Research: Catherine Bevan and Peter Morris
Production: Sevy Ribierre

Originated by Dot Gradations
Printed and bound in Hong Kong, China by South China Printing

ISBN 0 431 03919 4 (hardback)
07 06 05 04 03
10 9 8 7 6 5 4 3 2 1

ISBN 0 431 03924 0 (paperback)
08 07 06 05 04
10 9 8 7 6 5 4 3 2 1

British Library Cataloguing in Publication Data
Spilsbury, Louise and Spilsbury, Richard
Rivers. – (Wild Britain)
577.6'4'0941
A full catalogue record for this book is available from the British Library.

Acknowledgements

The Publishers would like to thank the following for permission to reproduce photographs: Bruce Colemann pp5, 13 (John Heseltine), 6 (Derek Croucher), 7 (Chris Gomersall), 10 (Franco Banfi), 17, 24 (Kim Taylor), 22 (Jane Burton), 25 (Paolo Fioratti); Corbis pp4 (Andrew Brown/Ecoscene), 9 (Julian Calder), 12 (Michael Boys), 14 (Hal Horwitz), 19 (Robert Pickett), 28 (Terence Nottingham), 29 (Adam Woolfitt); FLPA pp16 (B Borrell Casals), 18, 21 (Hugh Clark), 26 (Derek Middleton), 27 (Jurgen and Christine Sohns); NHPA pp8 (Stephen Dalton), 20, 23 (Lutra); Rex Features p11; SPL p15 (Simon Fraser).

Cover photograph of the start of the River Breamish, Northumberland, reproduced with permission of National Trust Photographic Library (John Darley).

The publishers would like to thank Michael Scott for his assistance in the preparation of this book.

Every effort has been made to contact copyright holders of any material reproduced in this book. Any omissions will be rectified in subsequent printings if notice is given to the Publisher.

Contents

Any words appearing in the text in bold, **like this**, are explained in the Glossary.

What is a river?

This is a view of the River Wye in Wales as it flows down the Wye valley.

A river is flowing water that moves towards the sea, a lake or another river. Many rivers start high in hills and mountains. The water is rain or melted snow.

A river habitat like this provides food and **shelter** for many different plants and animals.

A **habitat** is the natural home of a group of plants and animals. In this book we will look at some of the plants and animals that live, grow and **reproduce** in a river habitat.

Types of river

The water in this river moves quickly. Most plants or animals that tried to live here would get washed away.

When a river flows down a steep hill, the water moves quickly. As it rushes along, it carries stones and soil from the ground with it.

This river moves slowly. Many plants and animals live here.

When a river moves over flatter ground the water goes more slowly. More plants and animals can live in gentle rivers like these.

Changes

Swallows fly over rivers in summer. They catch insects in their beaks and drink the water.

In spring and summer, flowers grow in the warm sunshine. This is when animals have young so the river is a busy place. Birds come to eat the **insects** and the fish.

In the winter, many plants die back. Some parts stay alive underground, waiting to grow again in spring.

In winter, animals avoid the cold. Some insects rest in holes in trees or underground. Fish stay among the rocks on a **riverbed**. Many birds **migrate** to warmer places.

Living there

Most water plants have roots to hold them in place. Some **insects** hide among plants to stop being washed away.

It is not easy to live in water that is always moving. Many river plants grow **roots** into the **riverbed** to hold themselves in one place.

This otter lives in the riverbank. It hunts in the water for fish to eat.

Animals that live in a river have to be good swimmers. Fish swim by moving their tails and **fins**. River **mammals**, such as otters and mink, have **webbed feet** to swim with.

Plants on the riverbank

This riverbank has lots of plants growing along it. The plants just next to the water are mosses.

Plants live in different places in a river **habitat**. Some plants grow along the **riverbank**. Plants like moss and ferns grow best in damp places.

River animals often live among the roots of trees along riverbanks.

Trees that grow along the river's edge have **roots** that can live in very wet soil. These strong roots hold the tree up. They also stop water washing the soil away from the riverbank.

Plants in the water

The milfoil plant has tall stems. They grow up from the riverbed towards the light.

Plants need light to grow. Most plants catch light with their leaves. Plants that grow **roots** in the **riverbed** have long **stems** that hold leaves up to the light.

Many small river animals, like water snails, eat underwater plants like algae.

Algae are kinds of plant that grow on rocks and stones in the riverbed. Algae do not have leaves like other plants. Algae look like green slime and make rocks on the riverbed feel slippery.

River insects

Young caddis flies make cases of tiny stones or sticks to hide in while they grow.

Most river **insects** start life underwater. They **hatch** out of **eggs**. They stay in the gravel on the **riverbed** until they are fully-grown. Most young insects eat tiny bits of plant in the water.

After an adult mayfly, like this one, leaves the water, it does not feed. This is because it only lives for a few hours.

Some insects, like water beetles, stay in the river when they are fully grown. Mayflies and caddis flies leave the water when they are adults. They live in the air.

On the riverbed

This crayfish uses its claws to catch and eat small animals.

Many small animals live among the rocks and plants on the **riverbed**. Crayfish hide under stones. They come out at night to eat snails, worms and tiny fish.

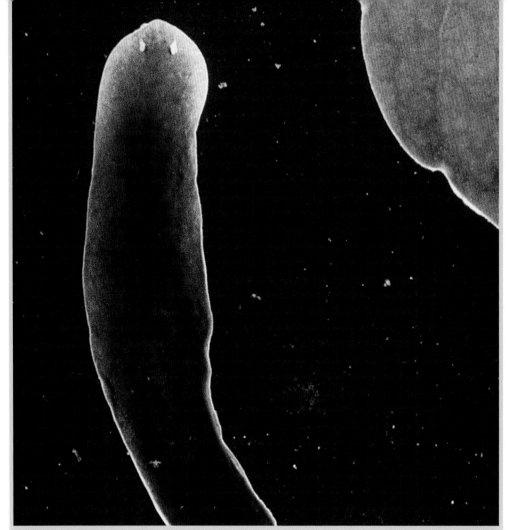

Animals like this flatworm float deep in the river. They eat tiny bits of dead plants and animals in the water.

When river plants and animals die they break up into very tiny bits. Some animals on the riverbed, like shrimp and flatworms, eat these bits as food.

River fish

Pike hide among water plants and dart out suddenly to catch fish with their many sharp teeth.

Many river fish feed on young **insects**. Some fish, like minnows and trout, eat plants, worms and snails. Some large fish, like salmon and pike, catch and eat other fish.

This brown trout has a dark back so that birds flying above the water cannot see it easily.

Many river birds eat fish. Some fish have dark coloured or speckled backs to help them hide in the water. This means that when they swim, it is harder for birds to see them.

Fish young

Trout lay their eggs in the gravel on the riverbed. The young hatch out after two months and swim off.

Fish **reproduce** by laying **eggs**. The young fish grow inside the eggs until they are ready to **hatch** out. Many river fish lay eggs among the sand or stones on the **riverbed**.

Perch lay their eggs in long threads among river plants.

Some fish lay their eggs among plants. This hides the eggs from other fish that might eat them. When the young fish hatch out, they are hidden among the water plants.

River birds

Ducks dip their heads underwater to eat plants.

Some birds live in **trees** near a river. They visit the river to drink water and find food. Some birds, like ducks and swans, use their **webbed feet** to paddle across the water.

Kingfishers hold their wings tight against their bodies. They dive deep underwater to catch food.

Some birds dive under the water. Kingfishers dive to catch fish in their sharp beaks. Dippers flap their wings to move underwater to eat snails and fish.

Voles and otters

Water voles mostly eat plants that grow in the water.

Water voles dig out **burrows** in the
riverbank. They live in the burrows and
come out to feed. They paddle along
underwater using their legs.

Otters use their claws to hold the slippery fish they eat.

Otters are the biggest river **mammals** living in Britain. Otters mainly eat fish, frogs and water birds, like coots and ducks. Otters live in holes in the riverbank.

Dangers

River animals may die if they get trapped inside these old tins and bottles.

Some people throw rubbish into rivers. Waste from factories also sometimes ends up in rivers. Plants and **insects** die in dirty river water. If they die, the animals that eat them may die too.

Many farmers keep a path of wild plants between rivers and fields to stop fertilizer getting into the water.

Sometimes rain washes soil or **fertilizers** from fields into rivers. Soil can make the water dirty. Fertilizers are chemicals that can cause **pollution**. Pollution damages river wildlife.

Food chain

All plants and animals in a river **habitat** are connected through the food they eat. Food chains show how different living things are linked. Here is one example:

The otter eats the crayfish.

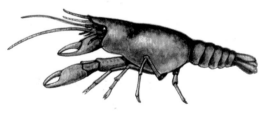

The crayfish eats the river snail.

The river snail eats bits of plants underwater.

The artwork on this page is not to scale.

Glossary

burrows holes in the ground that animals dig out to live in or have their young in

egg shell that some baby animals grow inside before they hatch out

fertilizer sprays farmers sometimes use to make crops grow well

fin a strong flap of skin on the back, sides or belly of a fish which helps it to swim

habitat the natural home of a group of plants and animals

hatch to be born from an egg

insect small animal that has six legs when an adult

mammals group of animals that feed their babies on milk. They have hair on their bodies.

migrate when animals move to a warmer place for the winter

pollution when air, water or land is poisoned, damaged or spoiled

reproduce when plants and animals make young just like themselves

riverbank sloping ground along the edge of a river

riverbed bottom of the river, where stones lie

roots parts of a plant that grow in the soil

shelter somewhere safe to stay, live and have young

stem the stalk that holds up the leaves and flowers of a plant

webbed feet when an animal has skin between the fingers or claws on its feet

Index